THE

LITTLE BLACK BOOK

FOR

INTERNS

(NAVIGATING THE HOLLYWOOD MAZE)

THE

LITTLE BLACK BOOK

FOR

INTERNS

(NAVIGATING THE HOLLYWOOD MAZE)

BY DOLCE VITA

FIRST EDITION

_____

_____

ISBN 1440457220

For my partner, family, and friends who give me the will to rise every morning and for their undying support, encouragement, shared stories and laughter.

Quote from "Jerry Maguire"

Dicky Fox: "The key to this business is
personal relationships."

CONTENTS

ACKNOWLEDGMENTS

The author wishes to thank her partner for being her rock throughout the years and for sharing tears and laughter throughout the peaks and valleys of this shared journey. The author also wishes to thank all of the interns that she has encountered for all of their efforts and friendship. Finally, the author wishes to thank all of her colleagues since she has learned a great deal from them and the precious few who have become close friends, part of an inner circle, where ideas, strategies, war stories and words of encouragement have been shared.

INTRODUCTION

The reason I have written this book is to share information I wish someone had shared with me when I began my professional endeavors in the entertainment industry. Consider this book like a letter from a friend who wishes you a good journey on what can be a tricky, slippery slope. There are many common pitfalls, but hopefully this book will give you guidance to avoid most of them. Currently, I live in Los Angeles, California and work in the entertainment industry. I prefer to remain anonymous as

I would like to have longevity in this industry.

I too began as an intern and part of what I do now is recruit interns. Consider the information I will share as an *attitude armor* you can wear as you take the steering wheel in your internship and beyond. I have pondered the question over and over in my mind as to why the attraction exists to work in the entertainment industry when it is widely-known that it is a place where you usually have to swim with the sharks and as in the animal kingdom, only the strong (or maybe I should say) sly survive. And my response to myself is simply this… That I get a kick out of the adrenaline rush that comes with the day in, day out drama of working behind-the-scenes so to speak and I get a thrill out of negotiating a great deal, or at times, helping my department or boss land that great deal!

Just as I have found what makes me tick in my chosen profession, you should ask yourself the same question. Maybe the answers vary or change over time. It may be that you realize that being part of an industry that churns out stories for the silver screen that speak to people, can be powerful and fulfilling. Or, the answer may be that you enjoy knowing that part of what you do actually helps an artist marry his/her work with business and it helps bring this artist's work to light for the enjoyment of many people.

You may even justify that you want to learn how to navigate the business side in order to gain enough knowledge to bring your own artistic work to light. If it is the latter, I encourage you not to remain behind-the-scenes too long. Your time will be better spent honing your artistic skills and creating a body of work that can help launch your career. Let the behind-the-scenes experts help you reach your dreams. After all, it is their job to find talented people with the potential to generate box office revenue or garner awards, which eventually generate the revenue. Money makes the world go 'round. What can I say?

Whatever answer you come up with, make certain that it is a positive one for you. The answer should motivate you to wake up in the morning, dash out the door to encounter the day's challenges for as long as you remain in your chosen profession. Feel free to navigate the book by chapter topic. (For this book's purposes, I will refer to Supervisor as *her*).

You may think that a lot of the information is obvious and you have heard it all before. Yet, I have encountered so many bright interns falling into the same pitfalls over and over that I figured a good reminder of dos and don'ts wouldn't hurt. As you read, I hope you find something of value to help you navigate and enjoy your journey.

Interview

(Do Your Research)

Make certain that you show up to the interview on time. I have found that map questing addresses is quite useful. If for some reason, you are running behind schedule, call your interviewer at least fifteen minutes ahead to state your reason whether it be that you are stuck in traffic, have gotten a flat tire, are lost or whatever the valid reason is. Do not make the mistake of not calling or of calling after your scheduled time to convey this message. This will automatically dock points against you in the selection process. I don't like to sound like a preacher, but I feel compelled to share this piece of advice as I have seen this oversight happen time and again.

Before you arrive to the interview, make sure you have done some research on what the company is about and learn about its mission, products, clients and goals. Also, take a look at their board members and personnel. If you know someone there, ask if they can put in a good word for you. This can land you on the short list of candidates to consider for the internship and may even lead you to a permanent position at the company.

One of the main questions you will most certainly be asked at the interview is, "Why do you want to work/intern for this company?" You better have a compelling reason. If you appear unmotivated during the interview, your interviewer(s) will also become unmotivated to hire you. When you give your compelling reason, make sure it falls in line with the position that you are applying for.

For example, if you are applying to be the Assistant to the Executive Director, do not state that what you really want to do is be a paid screenwriter.

That would immediately disqualify you. The recruiter wants to feel confident that the person she will hire will remain in the position for at least one year, and hopefully grow with the company.

In addition, make certain that you are dressed professionally and have groomed yourself that day. By that I mean do not go into the interview looking as if you are headed to the beach or have been working on your yard or your car. If you do so, you will be perceived as a slacker and who wants to hire someone like that? It foreshadows horror stories of others having to pick up the pieces that this candidate will most certainly leave behind. If you are male, and do not wear a well-groomed beard, make certain that you arrive clean-shaven.

The following applies to both sexes… Do not wear too much perfume or cologne. To be on the safe side, do not wear any at all. You do not want to give any reason of being offensive and be disqualified for this detail.

Another important note to keep in mind during the interview is to not speak ill of your former employers or co-workers. It will only make the interviewer think that this is what will be expected of you once you leave the company. Also, bring extra copies of your resume. From the start, make it convenient for the recruiter to want to hire you. Arriving empty-handed will dock your points. It conveys the message that you are unprepared.

Finally, after the interview, it is a good idea to email or mail in a *thank you* note. Usually, these details are noted and earn you those extra bonus points. Also, if a week or two goes by without hearing a word from the recruiter, feel free to call to learn the status of their search. This will reinforce the notion that you are still

interested in the position and
are looking forward to working
with the company.

BE PREPARED

Be prepared to come into your internship as if you were on a paid job assignment. You are there to assist your immediate supervisor and whoever else your supervisor has bestowed upon you. This is the first impression you are creating for yourself on your career track, and your performance here can set the tone for a successful journey. It is no secret that some of the tasks you may be handed may appear menial. However, when you perform those tasks be it, filing, running errands, picking up lunch, etc. you are being judged on your efficiency, flexibility, reliability, and calm and cool demeanor.

This is your opportunity to strut your stuff so to speak and demonstrate that you are a highly-competent team-player that will do whatever it takes to get the job done and make your supervisor's life easier. Make yourself so invaluable that your supervisor will not be able to imagine life without you. This can land huge rewards such as an exemplary letter of recommendation, job referral or job offer. Don't take menial tasks for granted!

As you maneuver day in and day out, remember to be helpful and pro-active. When you are being trained, do not expect a lot of hand-holding from your supervisor. She may usually give you the training/overview once and I highly recommend that you take notes. You may think that you are bright enough to retain the information, but usually there is a lot of information covered and there is no way that you will remember certain details such as codes to copiers, passwords on the computer or on-line UPS shipping systems, to name a few. There is nothing more inconvenient for your supervisor then having to repeat basic information such as the above especially with a busy schedule.

This reminds me of an incident at one of my organization's biggest fundraising events where I had one of my interns with me. She was my "shadow" which basically is our way of referring to a right-hand assistant on-site. She asked me for a pencil, and I looked at her sternly and said, "An assistant is always prepared." From that moment, she went on to become one of my star interns and I gave her a raving job referral when she needed it.

One of the things to keep in mind is that we are all

assisting someone whether it is our supervisor or our supervisor's supervisor or simply another co-worker. My motto is, "If you are not helping the process, you are hindering it." If you fall in the category of helping the process, you will become valuable in the eyes of many. This can put you on that fast track to success.

BE ON TIME

I can not emphasize enough how important it is to make it a habit to arrive to the office on time. You may try to justify that arriving fifteen or thirty minutes late is no big deal especially if your supervisor normally does not arrive on time or is usually at meetings outside the office in the mornings. It is especially important for you to be on time even when your supervisor is on the road or traveling... She may need to call in and reach reliable you for a phone number, conference her into a call or ask you to map quest an address for directions.

If you constantly arrive late, you will be perceived as unreliable, unprofessional and not serious about your career path. Plus, if you are there and always reachable in times of need, your value meter will continue to go up. Do not think because your supervisor isn't normally on time, you have permission to do so as well. If this is the trait of your supervisor, I am certain that she has earned that benefit. Continue to be on time as that will send a clear message that you are serious about the job. As you move up the ladder, you

will be setting an example to
your subordinates.

BE PRO-ACTIVE

Don't be lazy. This may sound quite basic, but I have seen this characteristic over and over... Don't expect things to be handed to you on a silver platter. You are there to serve, and not be served.

For example, if your supervisor gives you the simple task of mailing a letter or shipping a parcel, don't ask your supervisor for shipping supplies. Hopefully, on day one, you will have learned where the supply room is. If not, take it upon yourself to figure it out and get the necessary supplies you need without having to take it from your supervisor or her desk. Your supervisor has placed her supplies at her quick reach for her own convenience.

There is nothing more inconvenient than being wiped out of supplies unexpectedly! If you really want to earn extra bonus points, keep your supervisor's desk replenished with supplies and stationary. This will make her life easier and she will value you more for it.

KNOW YOUR PRIORITIES

On this point, I want to emphasize that you should always focus on your supervisor's needs first before you think about lending assistance to others in the company. I know this may sound odd to mention, but I have seen this occur and figured it best to state this observation. Since we work in social environments it is common that others in the company may ask you for assistance. Do not make the mistake of putting your supervisor on hold in order to take care of somebody else's request(s). This will send a

24

loud signal to your supervisor that you do not know where your priorities lie.

To expand on this topic, also pay close attention to the instructions you are given during the day. If you are informed that something needs to be mailed or shipped by 4:00 p.m. that day, do not set that mailing aside and wait for the last minute to take care of it. You never know what other projects will need your attention that day and you may even forget to meet your mail/shipment deadline. If this happens to you, you will not be looked upon too kindly. It will definitely dock your points on

the reliability meter, and you
do not want that to happen.

FIX YOUR MISTAKES ASAP

(Admit It If You're Wrong)

If you become aware that you have made a mistake, it is best to admit it as soon as you are aware of it, especially if rectifying it is of a timely essence. When you admit it, also think of ways you can resolve the mishap. Did you miss a messenger pick up? Then, offer to drop off the package yourself. Did you send out a UPS shipment to the wrong address? You can call UPS with the correct address and re-route the package.

If you take this approach, your supervisor will appreciate your honesty, and even more, will appreciate that you are offering solutions. This will definitely increase her confidence in you. Everybody makes mistakes, but it is how you handle a mistake that is most important. Be accountable and offer solutions. Your supervisor will appreciate you more for it!

LOOK, LISTEN, AND LEARN

Everyday you have an opportunity to learn not only from your supervisor, but from everyone around you. Keep your eyes and ears especially open to those that are the high achievers in the organization. You can learn a lot from them. Look and listen to everything… How they dress, how they walk and talk.

Notice that there is a certain, common thread among them… Notice that they dress in a manner that is professional, but not over-the-top. Their wardrobe usually says, "I'm taking care of business and I roll up my sleeves to pitch in whenever necessary." The way they walk is usually bold and self-confident as if to say, "I'm on board this moving train." And the way they talk is always confident with great listening skills and the ability to come up with solutions and put fires out quickly when necessary.

They consider the client as king and will do everything in their power to keep the client happy. This is especially a valuable asset as we all want our clients/ sponsors to return year after year for more business. Also, notice the way in which they handle other colleagues. This can easily be considered an art form. They usually have a manner that motivates, inspires and/or propels others into action.

This is quite a powerful quality especially when you need a team of people working with you for the success of an idea/campaign that you created or your supervisor has entrusted you with. The positive outcome of the campaign will not only make you look good, but it will make your supervisor look good. This can mean growth opportunities for you! Hello? Fast track!

On a side note, you can also learn from how shall I put this delicately? You can learn from the under-achievers or as a movie once labeled them "Clock-Watchers." You'll notice how they usually perform with what I call "B.M." which means a "bare minimum" approach. You usually know that they are just taking up space and energy at their jobs and are not fully-vested in the company's objectives. They are the ones who usually receive minimal raises, if any, and most certainly, no promotions.

You do not want to fall into this category unless you enjoy spending your hours, days, and what can dreadfully become wasted years at a dead-end situation for yourself. Do yourself a favor, and if you find yourself in this dreariness, make a life change. Allow your employer to fill the position with someone who is fully-vested and I am certain you will also be happier to follow a new and rewarding path.

BE RESOURCEFUL

You can be resourceful by paying attention to the current goals of the company. Is the company in the process of developing or modifying its website? Is the company looking to develop new relationships with certain Fortune 500 companies? If you happen to learn what those goals are from your immediate supervisor, or if you have the type of relationship with your supervisor where you can ask her about them, go for it. You will impress on her that you are inquiring so that you can lend any assistance to help the company reach its goals.

Your assistance can be in the manner of research. Research is a task easily achievable by the beautiful World Wide Web! Some of the research you may think about compiling are for example, links to websites that your company is interested in mimicking. Or, it can be compiling a contact list of executives of certain Fortune 500 companies that your company is interested in developing business relationships with. Even if you have to do this research on your own time, it will demonstrate to your supervisor that you are willing to go above and beyond the call of duty. That will definitely earn you some extra bonus points!

On another note, do not fall into the *whiner* or *complainer* category. As you spend a few years in your professional path, you will encounter those that fall into this category. Oh, you know who they are. They are the ones who feel like victims in their jobs. Things never run smooth enough for them, or the tools available may never be enough or the *right ones*.

They always seem to think that the *Solution Fairy* should pay a visit to them to resolve the issues of the day. But guess what? Each and every one of us *IS* the *Solution Fairy*. It can take one ordinary person regardless of title in the office to verbalize a problem and offer a logical solution for the issue to be resolved. It can be as easy as that.

One example I would like to share is this… Our marketing department is a hard working department with many on-going projects with high priorities for the organization. We have known for a while that we need to take advantage of free online opportunities to promote our live events. Basically, we have needed to create a presence online via social networks such as MySpace and Facebook. Well, this wasn't happening soon enough so one of the assistants took it upon herself to create the online presence on the above mentioned websites. Problem solved. Remember… "If you are not helping, you are hindering the process."

BE RELIABLE

If your supervisor gives you a project and has especially emphasized a due date, do not allow the due date to pass without completing the assignment. If you are having trouble with the project alert your supervisor early enough so that she can help you with resources such as other co-workers or technological tools you may need to complete the task. Do not allow time to pass while you remain in a holding pattern. That is not only a waste of your time but of your supervisor's time as well.

Early alerts allow for enough time to come up with a solution or different approach. It is very disappointing to give a special assignment to an intern to then learn upon the due date that the project is nowhere near completion. From that moment on, your supervisor will think twice, if at all, in giving you any assignments that may contribute to growth opportunities for you.

IMPROVING PROCESSES

If your supervisor gives you a project, and you believe there is a more efficient way of achieving better results, you may want to share that idea with her. This has always been a welcoming aspect in my book. However, there are supervisors who feel intimidated by better ideas. If you feel your supervisor falls into this category, it is better not to rock the boat. Go with the flow. Proceed as instructed and achieve the best results possible under the circumstances.

A final note about supervisors who are easily intimidated... It is unfortunate, but you will encounter such supervisors. I personally view these types of supervisors as having an insecurity complex. Don't take their negative remarks or lack of enthusiasm for your ideas personally.

The best supervisors I have found are those who are self-confident and empower their subordinates to grow. Because of their ability to empower, this encourages better ideas and creates growth not only for subordinates, but for the supervisor and organization as well. It's a win-win situation...

Seek to work for such supervisors as this can put your career on the fast track to success.

BEHAVIOR AFTER HOURS

(Guard Your Reputation)

Chances are that you will work at an event for your company that is after normal business hours. Just because you are at this event and there is alcohol being served, it does not give you the permission to partake and become inebriated. Keep in mind that you are officially on duty and even if you were not, you should always behave in a professional manner as you are being looked upon as a representative of the company. I have seen many a bright intern do very well at the office, but then come time for an after-hours event, they forget about maintaining that professional demeanor.

You may think, "Well, I've heard of certain executives who misbehave at the parties and they continue to do well or even get promoted." And as you've probably heard, "Hollywood is the only place where you can fail upward." Keep in mind that those misbehaving executives who can get away with their behavior usually fall within the 1% of the "untouchables" list. By "untouchables" I mean they are star performers in the industry who usually reap great box office revenues or something major to that effect, and everyone turns the other way when they misbehave because it would be a detriment to their company to not have them on the payroll. Believe me, if you are reading this book, you do not fall within that 1%.

It is common for companies to place star interns on a short list toward a permanent position and I am saddened to say, that there have been occasions where I have not given a positive review to an intern for consideration of a permanent position due to their behavior after hours. Well, you might say that I am a stuffy fuddy duddy. However, keep in mind that when you refer someone, that referral is a reflection on you. If one continually refers candidates that can not deliver or behave inappropriately, ones own opinion will quickly become diminished.

BE TRUSTWORTHY

(Beware Of Gossip)

It is important that if you want to be considered trustworthy, that you do not share confidential information that has been disclosed to you. Be it information that your supervisor, or other personnel have shared with you. Believe me if you share this information, the news will quickly spread through the office and you will not be perceived as trustworthy. There have been studies disclosing that it is not human nature to maintain secrets. Keeping secrets can actually cause stress. So fight against this human inclination and know that once you tell one person, it is no longer a secret! Consider it office news or gossip.

Usually when gossip spreads, people share their source as well, which means, you can be perceived as a big mouth. Not only is it a bad image for you, but from then on it is unlikely that you will remain in people's confidence which means less information for you. And as the saying goes, "Information is power."

This reminds me of an unfortunate situation I witnessed. There was a star performer in a company who innocently shared some information about a co-worker. She didn't think the information was confidential or any big deal. It may have been something related to this person's current romance status such as a break-up… Needless to say, the person she confided this information to secretly disliked her because she had recently begun to outshine her at work. This "confidant" then went and informed the person who had mentioned his break up. The incident then landed on the ears of the star performer's supervisor.

Soon afterward, this star performer's approval meter took a nose dive. As it turns out, even her supervisor secretly disliked her because she was intimidated by this employee's quick ascent within the company. Needless to say, the supervisor used the incident along with any other little mishaps she could dig up in order to diminish the star's popularity in the office.

It got to the point that this star performer experienced such an icy environment that it weighed heavy on her. It became so unbearable that she felt it best to leave, even if it meant, leaving without unemployment benefits. You may say, "Well, it was inevitable because this star was becoming unpopular even in the eyes of her supervisor." However, if the star wouldn't have disclosed this confidential information, her exit could have at least been delayed to the point where she could have secured a new opportunity without having to take such a leap of faith. That leap probably was not only emotionally painful, but a strain on her bank account as well. Double whammy! On this point I'd like to emphasize, "Don't take such a leap, unless you know you are a good swimmer."

BEWARE OF WHAT YOU WRITE IN EMAILS

The reason I want to emphasize this point, is again, from an incident I witnessed. There was an assistant to the Executive Director who was new on the job and she wrote a sarcastic remark about her supervisor. By mistake, she pushed "Reply All" on the First Class email application, and the email went out to the entire staff. I empathized and quickly showed her how to hit the "Unsend" button on the email application. Unfortunately, for staff that use a Blackberry or

Treo, the "Unsend" option does not apply.

Our Executive Director owns a Treo, and to this assistant's detriment, it meant that the Executive Director was able to read the email. Needless to say, the Assistant was not at work the next day. I guess, the old motto applies, "If you aren't going to say something nice, don't say anything at all."

BEWARE OF WHAT YOU SAY IN PUBLIC

The reason I bring this up is to bring up another major mishap that I witnessed. There was another assistant who was the assistant to the Executive Director of the organization. For the most part, most of the staff did not have this assistant in their good graces. One major flaw he had was that he easily disclosed confidential information such as staff salaries, his supervisor's personal rendezvous, and more. Since his supervisor had really taken a liking to him she shielded him as much as possible from staff complaints.

However, on one major occasion, this assistant was under the influence of a chemical substance and he criticized his supervisor to the press that was attending one of the company's major events. This was overheard by the company's publicist, and soon afterward, this assistant was terminated. On the same topic, I want to state that even if you are off hours and you run into a co-worker or former co-worker on the weekend, do not run your mouth criticizing your current employer or colleagues.

You do not know where your listener's loyalties are and there is a great possibility that what you disclose will land in several co-worker's ears come Monday morning. The gossip may even land in your employer's ears and we all know what can happen soon afterward. And on this point I will emphasize the opposite of the Nike commercial, "Just Don't."

DON'T DIP YOUR NIB IN THE OFFICE INK

Basically, it is standard knowledge that it is not a good idea to get involved in romantic relationships at the office although studies show that this is becoming a growing occurrence. There are several reasons why this is not a good idea. One is that if it becomes public knowledge, supervisors can get the impression that the parties involved in the relationship are not really serious about their career or are not focused during work hours.

If one of the parties involved is a direct supervisor of the other party, co-workers may believe that favoritism comes into play for certain appealing projects or promotions. So even if company policy allows for employees to date, normally it is not perceived in a positive light. And, if there is a relationship between an employee and an intern, the perception is even worse.

If you are strongly considering entering into a romantic relationship at the office, be prepared for the worse which is to leave the company if the relationship sours. It is highly unlikely that you will be able to remain level-headed while going through a romantic break-up at the office. But, you never know? You may be one of the lucky few we sometimes read about who finds romance at the office and one or both parties leaves the company and the couple ends up getting married. Sometimes fairy tales do come true. (But, don't count on that too much).

SHARING IDEAS

One way to obtain positive notice is when you have ideas that are either creative or are effective in helping the company reach its goals. If you are afraid that your supervisor or someone else in the company will steal your ideas or take all the credit, one easy thing you can do is to share your ideas within a group of people. This will definitely ensure that people will be aware that you are the originator of the ideas. If you continually come up with great ideas, this can definitely earn

you more extra bonus points. You
always want them wanting more!

NETWORK

(Work It and Work It)

As you spend time in your internship, and hopefully you are spending lunch time with others in the office, feel free to communicate what your long-term plans are. Whether your plans are to land a permanent position at the same company, another company or enter an advanced educational program, chances are that those you are communicating with will be able to give you advice, a referral or other valuable information. It is important that you remain in people's good graces because if they perceive you as earnest and worthy, they will want to take you under their wing or give you information that can help guide you in your career path.

When networking with outside company contacts beware not to overstep any boundaries. An example of this is something that happened at one of my organization's events. There was a panel discussion with the standard question and answer session with the audience. However, soon after the discussion was over, one of our interns approached one of the panelists to pawn off his script. The director of the event noticed this, and black-listed this intern from "working" at future events. This was a shame since this particular intern had demonstrated eagerness and great effort in the office.

Keep in mind that some of the most valuable contacts you will make are actually the people you are already sitting next to. In the industry people shift quite frequently from company to company and can move quickly up the ladder. In time, you will be pleasantly surprised to realize that you have built quite a helpful rolodex of important contacts that can help get you in the door. Be patient.

Accept as many invitations as you can to parties, weddings, bar mitzvahs, house warmings, etc. Any opportunity for you to be in social contact with the people in your industry is a good thing. You never know who you are going to meet or what new piece of information you can learn.

You should consider signing up to receive email alerts for various network groups. This can keep you up to date on new trends, hot topics, and new ideas. New relationships can form that can help you to

further your career. Be active,
not reactive!

NETWORKING RESOURCES

The word "network" should not be a negative connotation. Simply view it as being social and making your contacts aware that you still exist and how talented you are. Keep in mind that there are many networking platforms online such as MySpace and Facebook. You may wonder, "Is that networking?" Yes! Keeping in touch and remaining on people's radar is networking!

There have been articles published and television interviews given where recruiters have mentioned that part of their process in screening candidates is to search for candidates' profiles on the online social networks such as the above mentioned. If the candidate appears to be too much of a *party animal*, so to speak, that can raise a red flag. As mentioned before, image is important. A good online networking platform is LinkedIn.

Although I have been happily employed, I made it known to my employer that I was using that online service to reach out to international contacts that may have been too difficult to reach otherwise. At first, my employer seemed skeptical on my reason since the first obvious reason to use this service is to seek employment. However, I printed letters from my international contacts that also sang LinkedIn's praises in helping people connect. I am happy to state that as of writing about this topic, LinkedIn has now become a sponsor for my organization. Can you tell that I am a believer in LinkedIn? If you are not a subscriber, I highly recommend it!

KEEPING IN TOUCH

(The Industry Thrives on Referrals)

Once you finish your internship, keep in touch with your supervisor. This falls in line with the saying, "The squeaky wheel gets the oil." If you complete your internship on a positive note and you are in your supervisor's good graces, keep in touch to remain fresh on her mind. This way she will think about you when a position opens up or will refer you when she learns of an opening in another department or company.

Usually department heads look out for each other and they share information on star candidates. The entertainment industry thrives on referrals! Also, keep in mind that keeping in touch with people during moments when you do not need them is best, because that way it isn't so awkward to resurface out of the blue asking for a favor in a time of need.

LEARN THE LINGO &
WHO'S WHO
(Read the Trades)

Immerse yourself in the current events and learn who the movers and shakers in the industry are by reading the standard trades: "The Hollywood Reporter" and "The Daily Variety." You can read them online or you may find them available to read at a national chain bookstore. This will give you an idea on what the companies are about, what they are producing, who is hiring, who is moving up the ladder, etc. Remember, knowledge is power.

Also, you can research people in the industry on imdb.com or on the industry's official photographer websites such as wireimage.com or gettyimages.com. Look at the images of the people in the industry so that hopefully if you run into one of your icons, you can shake their hand at an event. You will be surprised to learn that many are accessible and may even give you their contact information if you approach them in a civilized and professional manner.

ATTEND INDUSTRY EVENTS

(Stay in the Loop)

If you live in Los Angeles, and hopefully you do, make it a point to attend as many public industry events as possible. This is a good way of obtaining an idea on what it takes to work in your desired profession and at the same time, meet the movers and shakers who usually participate on panels. Usually, it is free or nearly free to attend these events.

<u>Here are a few websites to get you started…</u>

Academy of Motion Pictures Arts & Sciences: Oscars.org

Writers Guild of America, west: WGA.org

Directors Guild of America: DGA.org

Screen Actors Guild: SAG.org

Film Independent: FilmIndependent.org

American Cinematheque: AmericanCinematheque.com

One final comment about living in Los Angeles… If you do not live in Los Angeles and do not have a Los Angeles phone number, you may be perceived as not serious about developing a career in the industry. I have heard about people getting around this issue by renting an L.A. P.O. Box and using a cell phone with an L.A. number (on the West side). Do whatever you have to do to give the impression you are living and working in the West side of Los Angeles.

DON'T TAKE IT PERSONAL
IF YOU DON'T GET HIRED

There are many reasons why you may not have been selected for the position you interviewed for. Don't take it personal. I realize that it is easier said than done, but I want to stress that there are many reasons why a person may not be selected for a position. One reason may be that your background may not fall in line with the organization or company's mission.

For example, if the organization has a mission to promote diversity, they may also be looking to fill their openings with candidates who have a diverse background. I know that this may sound like reverse-discrimination, but diversity is a growing initiative with many companies these days. Maybe it is a way to heal old wounds for lack of employment opportunities for minorities in the past. It may also be a way to continually obtain sponsorship by other companies who need to support organizations with diverse initiatives. Organizations with these initiatives usually have a grading system impressed upon Supervisors which is reflected upon their yearly review.

Basically, their Supervisor will grade them on how well they hire a diverse staff. However, I have found several other recurring reasons why a candidate is not hired.

I will list them below:

- Not the right fit for the culture of the company.
- Not persuasive enough during interview to demonstrate passion for the position.
- If the candidate was asked what their career goal would be in five years, and the candidate responded with a disconnect in their current path, that would be a red flag.

- The candidate voiced a current hobby or interest that gave the impression that their focus or energy would be taken away from the position.
- The candidate simply did not "click" personality-wise with the employer.
- At the end of the interview, the candidate declined parking validation because he/she doesn't own a car. (Many employers need their interns/ employees with cars in order to run errands or attend events).

YOUR DESK, YOUR CAR, YOUR IMAGE

I know this may sound like mommy reprimanding you or checking up on you, but it is a good idea to keep your desk and car neat. Let me just state that one day you may be asked to give your supervisor and/or department a ride to lunch or a meeting. It happens on occasion. And when that happens, don't you think you will be so proud of yourself to be able to provide a ride in a clean car without trash or items floating around on the floor or back seat? This will demonstrate you have your act together. There is nothing wrong with that when you are trying to climb up that ladder right?

The same applies for keeping a neat desk. It implies you are organized and focused. Some people even go to the length of not having personal items such as family photos on their desks. Some experts have speculated that if you have these items on your desk, you are not 100% focused on your job. It is up to you on how far you want to go. At the end of the day, what should really count is your performance on the job, but a positive image can also help.

BE NICE TO ASSISTANTS

(And Everyone Else Too!)

I can't emphasize this enough. First of all, my philosophy is to be nice to everyone. You know that old adage, treat people the way you want to be treated. Well, the same applies especially in the entertainment industry because today's assistant may be tomorrow's producer or what have you.

It is funny how people overlook networking with their own neighbor at work. Everybody knows somebody plus people move around all the time especially

in this industry. You just
never know. I have actually
experienced interns that come
through my door and soon enough
they give me a call to let me
know that they've landed
employment at a studio or
publicity firm. Sometimes they
have even offered me a position
at their companies! I call it
"As The World Turns."

WHERE TO SEEK INTERNSHIPS/EMPLOYMENT

Some of the main websites for the entertainment industry are Showbizjobs.com and Entertainmentcareers.net. There are also newcomers such as bizgigconnect.com, Mashable.com and Creativeheads.net to be aware of. For wider searches visit Monster.com, HotJobs.com, Indeed.com and SimplyHired.com. You should also conduct searches on individual studio or company websites as they usually have employment and internship opportunities listed.

There is also a job list available on a weekly basis called the UTA Job List. In order to obtain this job list you must be a USC student or alumnus or you can obtain the listing if your employer subscribes to it as a recruiter. Ask your employer or USC friends about it and more than likely they or someone they know will be able to forward it to you. Being able to obtain this list is perceived as winning that golden ticket in the Willy Wonka chocolate bar. Where there is a will, there is a way! Go get it!

Quote from "Jerry Maguire"

Dicky Fox: "Hey, I don't have all the answers. In life, to be honest, I failed as much as I have succeeded. But I love my wife. I love my life. And I wish you my kind of success."